The Red Monster

...and other evocative tales

By
Sudha Narasimhachar

Illustrated By
Parijat Suman

UNICORN BOOKS Pvt. Ltd.

Distributors
PUSTAK MAHAL

Publishers
UNICORN BOOKS, New Delhi-110002
E-mail: unicornbooks@vsnl.com
Website: www.unicornbooks.in • www.kidscorner.in

Distributors
Pustak Mahal, Delhi
J-3/16, Daryaganj, New Delhi-110002
☎ 23276539, 23272783, 23272784 • *Fax:* 011-23260518
E-mail: info@pustakmahal.com • *Website:* www.pustakmahal.com

Sales Centre
10-B, Netaji Subhash Marg, Daryaganj, New Delhi-110002
☎ 23268292, 23268293, 23279900 • *Fax:* 011-23280567
E-mail: rapidexdelhi@indiatimes.com

Branch Offices
Bangalore: ☎ 22234025
E-mail: pmblr@sancharnet.in • pustak@sancharnet.in
Mumbai: ☎ 22010941
E-mail: rapidex@bom5.vsnl.net.in
Patna: ☎ 3294193 • *Telefax:* 0612-2302719
E-mail: rapidexptn@rediffmail.com
Hyderabad: *Telefax:* 040-24737290
E-mail: pustakmahalhyd@yahoo.co.in

ISBN 81-780-6065-5

Edition : 2006

Printed at : Virgo Press, Delhi

Acknowledgement

Although a writer basically writes to express his/her feelings, he/she definitely wishes to be heard – or rather read. A writer needs a proper platform to exhibit the work. He/she is inspired to write more when his/her work is printed and published. I am indebted to my Bank, Canara Bank, where I first received this platform. The Bank holds annual literary contests and I was recognised for my creative writing year after year, which inspired me to write more.

Secondly, I was encouraged and inspired a lot by my mother, sisters and brother and many friends.

Thirdly, I wish to record my gratitude to Mr Joseph Kaval, who began a literary organisation *Kathalok*, bringing together local writers and encouraging us to take up writing seriously to become authors. Through *Kathalok* I was introduced to many writers and translators, who have been a great source of inspiration for me.

Above all, I must record my immense gratitude to my husband, who has always been supportive and assists me in all literary activities. He is my first reader and gives valuable suggestions.

And, of course, my children Varsha and Varun are always with me – reading, appreciating, constructively criticising, assisting in editing/correcting and sharing my joy of success and pain of failure. But for my entire family, I would have never been able to be sincere in my expressions.

I dedicate this book to each of these people because of whom I am seeing my first book in print.

—Sudha Narasimhachar

Contents

1

The Surprise Gift

Chinni. That was her previous name. Memories about her old self were safely locked in one corner of her heart. She could not forget those memories. Not that her present was not good enough for her to wipe out those memories, but certain memories are carved and leave permanent impressions in our hearts and for Jose, as she is called today, those memories of Chinni were such.

Jose tightened her seatbelt, as requested by the airhostess. Her English husband Robert too did the same. Their ten-year-old son Mike sat in the centre and tightened his seatbelt with his dad's help.

"Mom, I am too excited to visit India. I heard there are many beautiful historical monuments over there. Are we going to see any of them?"

"Sure Mike. We will visit a few of them. We are going on a long holiday. I am visiting India after 18 years. I am also excited. Robert, how many times have you gone to India?"

"I have gone to Delhi once on an official meet and three years ago, you know, I had gone to Calcutta along with Mr Chakraborthy to attend his sister's wedding. That was real fun, Jose. Indian weddings are full of fun and frolic."

"Mom! You said I have a surprise in India. What is it? I am too curious."

"Curiosity killed the cat! Surprises are fun Mike. You have to wait. Just a few more days."

The flight stabilised on the clear blue sky. Mike and Robert began their game of chess. Jose opened her box of thoughts.

Chinni, the weak, lanky, dark child was playing in the sand pit as usual. She had very few friends there. It was her experience that the person to whom she grew dear left her soon. It happened with Mariamma. She was such a sweet lady. She was round and plumpy and loud and cheerful. She loved all the kids there equally, whether they were cute and healthy like Tarun or weak and ugly like Chinni.

Chinni remembered how, in the afternoons, Mariamma would make them all sit on a bamboo mat and tell them interesting stories about gods, angels, animals and children. Very often she would hug them, cuddle and kiss them and put them on her cushiony lap. Chinni would feel warm and secure on her lap.

Suddenly, all that comfort was lost. Periamma announced in the assembly that Mariamma would not come anymore as she had joined God and asked them all to pray for her soul.

Then Chinni got closer to Vani. She was a very cute and quiet girl. She would never boss around. They both could play for hours together without any quarrel. She would share any eatable that she received from her relatives, who visited her once in a while. Yes. She had some relatives. Chinni would always feel jealous when people visited her friends at the ashram. Why didn't anybody come to see her? One day, she asked Periamma between sobs as to why nobody came to meet her.

"Chinni, why do you want anybody from outside to come and see you? I am here. Mariamma is here. All your friends are here. We all love you, child. Don't feel sad. God is with you always," Periamma pacified her.

Chinni could not understand what she meant by saying *God is with you always*. Where was He? Was she talking about those four-armed gods, travelling on various animals, or was she talking about that God Mariamma would talk about, who was brutally crucified? Chinni asked no questions.

The day Vani too left her was the most sorrowful day of her life. Vani and Chinni were playing in the tree house and Gowri came running: "Vani, Vani, Periamma is calling you. Come soon."

Vani climbed down the wooden stairs and Chinni too followed her with suspicion.

"You stay here Chinni. Vani will be back soon," Gowri the *ayah* said.

After they both left, she stealthily followed them to Periamma's room and overheard the talk going on inside. That was because Papu was separated from her in a similar way a few days ago. Intuition warned Chinni that something bad was about to happen.

Chinni could not follow anything as the conversation was in English and they spoke only Tamil.

Periamma then turned to Vani and said in Tamil: "Vani, this is Ravi uncle and Charu aunty. They would like to take you to their house. Say 'hello' to them."

Vani looked flabbergasted and immediately said *namaste* mechanically and then started crying. "No Periamma. I won't go anywhere. I want to stay with you all. I want Chinni and all the others."

"Vani. Don't cry. You are not going today. There is more time. This uncle and aunty will put you in a good school and buy you lot of toys. They will bring you here regularly. You can meet us often. If you go with them, you can become a doctor like Mahima aunty or a teacher like Lovely aunty. Don't you like that? Don't cry. Go and play."

That aunty gave Vani a big chocolate and a white teddy bear and hugged her. Tears rolled down her cheeks.

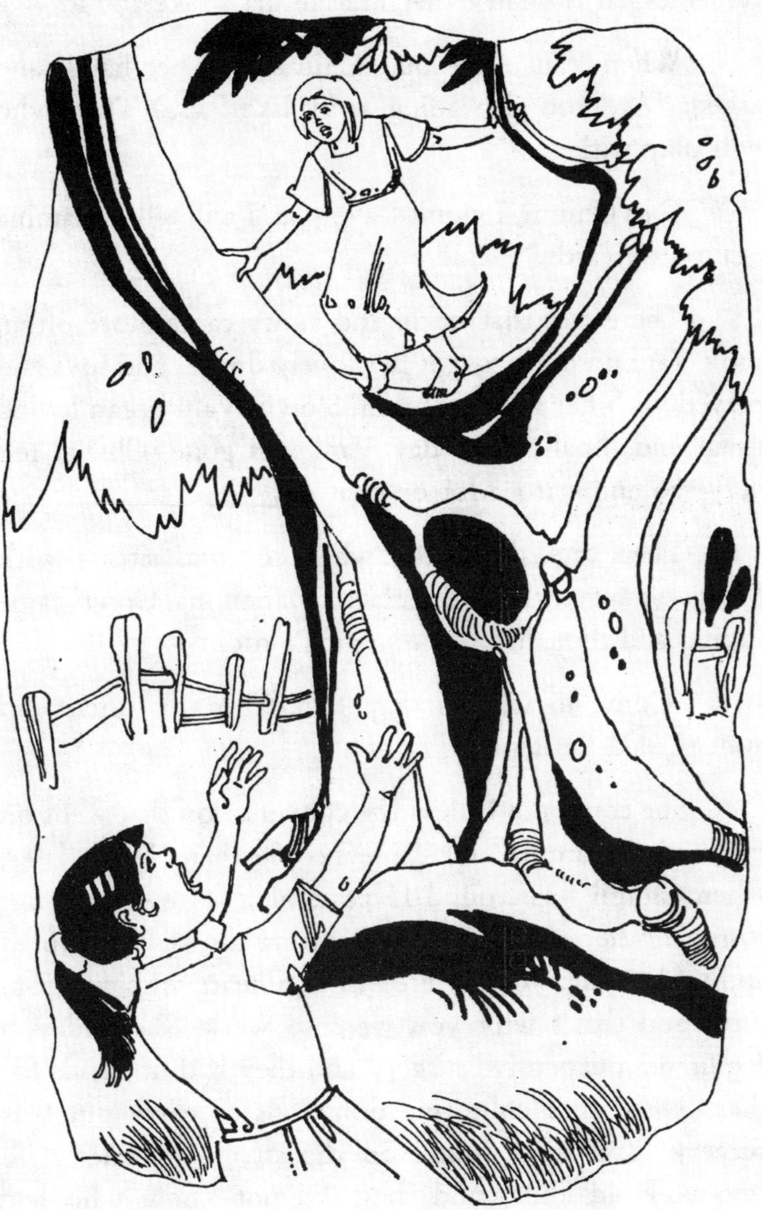

She was a very beautiful lady. On seeing her, Chinni remembered the fairy that Mariamma spoke about.

When Vani came out, Chinni held her hands and asked: "Are you also going away like Papu? Then who will play with me?"

"No Chinni, I won't leave you. I will tell Periamma again afterwards."

Thereafter that uncle and aunty came more often, took Vani on outings, got her lovely dresses and toys and played with her at the ashram. Slowly Vani began loving them and, finally, one day Vani was gone. Chinni felt very sad and cried a lot on that day.

Then one afternoon, when she was sitting with Mangala aunty, who had replaced Mariamma, Gowri came calling and took her to Periamma's room.

"Come in Chinni. Say 'hello' to this uncle and aunty," said Periamma.

She could not follow the conversation that went on between Periamma and those people then. Much later, when Chinni was around 15 years old, Susan – that's her foster mother – told her: "Periamma showed you to us and told us that you suffered from a heart problem from birth and that's why you were so weak. She said you required an expensive surgery and they had no funds for that. They were collecting donations to carry out that surgery. You were found on the street orphaned as a two-week-old child, and they did not know who had abandoned you. At that moment, your daddy and I decided that you would be our first child and brought you here, Jose. After the surgery, you picked up health and brought life into our barren lives. Jose, I love you!"

Jose wept her heart out on that day. It was almost eight years since she had been with Susan and George in Canada. They were so nice to her. Though they had two children later on, their first love was Jose and they never ever made her feel lonely or left out. When foster parents could be so affectionate, why did her own mother desert her?

Coming back to the days in the ashram, Chinni was thrilled on that day when Periamma told her that Susan aunty and George uncle were going to take her with them, though she did feel sad to leave Periamma and the others, because she thought if she stayed on, she would be the only one left in the ashram. Many of them were leaving one by one. How lucky she was that though she looked so ugly and weak, such fair and wealthy people were willing to take her.

A few days after that, when she got used to Susan and George, Chinni left the ashram with them. For the first time, she wore those blue trousers and yellow T-shirt, had her hair cut neatly and put on soft rubber shoes. She was thrilled to travel by the aeroplane, which she had only seen in the sky. That is how Chinni went to Canada and became Jose.

Jose did not disappoint her parents and did very well in studies. She graduated as a communication consultant and worked for a TV channel. It was there that she met Robert. He was a very nice guy. Their hearts met and they married. Jose had told Robert all about her past and also expressed her wish to go to the ashram where she grew up as a child.

Robert, Jose and Mike now entered that ashram at Chennai. Jose's heart began thumping loudly. Tears flowed down her cheeks automatically. The place had not changed even a bit, except that it had grown older. The bright coloured slide, seesaw and swing now looked almost colourless, covered with rust here and there.

Even the sand pit was still there. The tree house was in tatters. The building wore a sorry look with cracked walls and faded colours. Jose felt the kids looked hungry and not well attended. They entered the office room and found a middle-aged man with spectacles sitting there.

"Yes?" he said, a question mark on his weathered face.

"I am Jose. He is my husband Robert and this is our son Mike. We have come from Canada."

"Please sit down. What can I do for you?"

Jose told him all about herself and the purpose of her visit and asked, "Sir, if you don't mind, can I ask you a question?"

"Yes. Go ahead."

"The ashram looks like it needs a lot of attention. Is there any problem for funds?"

"Yes Madam. After Periamma's death, nobody in her family came forward to take care of this ashram. I used to assist her as a social worker and took over the reigns helplessly. I come from a very poor family. I left my clerical job and did not even marry, just to take care of these helpless children." He paused and then went on.

"But due to some legal problem created by Periamma's sons, we are unable to get government funds. I carry on only with voluntary donations. Being alone and suffering from cancer, I am unable to do much. I am not even admitting new entrants. But what can one do with the existing children and those dumped at our doorsteps stealthily?"

Jose felt very bad. She made up her mind to help the ashram in some way. By then, the peon went and fetched a little girl.

"What's your name sweetheart?" Jose asked.

After being prompted in Tamil by Mr Rao, the caretaker, the girl answered in a feeble voice, "Mala."

"She is here for the last three years. She is now six years old. Her father left her here, after her mother died of AIDS, since he too was suffering from AIDS. He is now battling for his life at the AIDS centre. This girl is affected by polio. Otherwise her health is fine. She is a very sweet child," explained Mr Rao.

"Mike, say 'hello' to Mala. She is your sister," said Jose.

Mike was surprised.

He looked at Mala and his mother. After a minute of silence, he said, "My sister? Are we going to take her along? How nice, Amma! Hello Mala!"

Mike extended his hand happily. Mala was confused and in tears. Jose was well aware of what was going on in her little mind and she knew how to handle that.

"Don't feel scared, Mala. I am your Amma," she said in broken Tamil, which she faintly remembered.

Robert and Jose made out a cheque for US $2000, promised more help on their return and took Mala with them... after a month.

"So, this is the surprise you were talking about Mom?" asked Mike excitedly on the return flight. "Yes son. This is it. Now, you are the big brother and you have to take care of your sis Mala with love. Will you?"

"Sure Mom. I love her so much. Let's first get her leg treated Mom," replied Mike.

"Thank you son. Thank you Robert." Jose pressed her husband's palm with affection.

❑❑❑

2

The Autobiography

I curl up further. It is so chilly tonight. It is raining too. So the whole place is very messy. My beautiful fluffy tail, which was white as snow, has become brown. Everyone in my pet master's house loved my tail and people who visited their place looked at it with awe. I roamed all evening to find this little shelter near the roadside hotel. I am very sad today.

Just a fortnight ago, I was in a secure place, with six people doting on me from morning till night. It was a majestic old mansion, with a lush green garden surrounding it. It had seven to eight big rooms upstairs and downstairs and I was free to go to any room, except the kitchen and the *pooja* room. My mistress was a loving old lady, who would call me by all sorts of pet names, as though I were her grandson! My name was actually Raja. Yes, that's how everybody else called me.

My mistress had a son Rahul Khanna, whose wife was Meena and children were Mona and Vikram. My master Khanna *Saab* was an old man always dressed in snow-white kurta pyjamas. He would take me on long walks twice a day. I would sit patiently when he met his walkmates and chatted for hours together. I could daydream and see all my friends and enemies on the street. I would walk proudly with my master when my friends on the street looked at me with envy. They probably envied my good build, shining healthy body and loving master. They would look dirty, skinny-whinny and scared. Though they would bark from a distance, they never dared do so near me!

I was fed tasty vegetarian food, vitamin biscuits, occasional sweets and bakery items. I was let free, except when some new visitors came. Never would I be allowed to go outside in such bad weather. Mona and Vikram would pester their Dada and get me inside. I would sleep comfortably on a soft sofa lying in the verandah. Once a week, Rahul *Saab* would bathe me lovingly, with a sweet-smelling soap and warm water.

In spite of such a comfortable life, sometimes I envied my friends on the street. I would think: they are free to go anywhere, eat anything and do any mischief, whereas I have always to listen to these people's instructions. I have no freedom to mingle with girlfriends or fight with those rowdies on the road. What a life! I would think. Never did I imagine that I would get what I wished for and then repent for having got it.

****

That day too was like any other day. Dada woke up fresh, tied the belt to my collar and took me out for a long walk. All the scenes on the way were the same. I met the same friends and foes and their masters. We sat in the park, where many people came to jog. Dada chatted with his friends as usual. After all this, we just had to cross a distance of a furlong to reach home.

Dada began crossing the road with me and zoom came that lorry and hit Dada before he could cross over. I had already crossed that point. Dada immediately fell with a thud and soon a pool of blood formed around him, but he still held my leash tightly. A lot of people gathered. I started wailing because Dada did not open his eyes or speak to me as usual. After some time Vikram, who was all in tears, came rushing and took us home after we had been there for long. Dada was lying down in my favourite verandah, without even moving. Many people came and cried a lot. Then they took away Dada somewhere. He never returned.

Nobody spoke to me for a few days, except the children. They did give me something to eat. But I was not in a mood to eat. I wanted to see Dada. I too cried.

After a few months passed like this, suddenly one day a big lorry came and all the things were loaded onto the lorry, including my sofa. Many people visited the house and a lot of discussions went on for days.

I heard my mistress talking about me to Rahul and he said: "What to do Amma? We are going abroad. We cannot take Raja along. Even for your visa I had to run around a lot. I have asked all my friends. No one wants to take Raja. I too feel miserable. But there is no other option. We will leave him here. If the new owners want, they can have him. Otherwise, fate will decide his future."

Daadima cried a lot. She petted me a lot for the last one week and fed me all my favourite food items. A fortnight ago, all of them got into a big car. I sensed something and started getting tensed up. I ran hither and thither. The whole house was empty. I felt very sad. All of them were crying. They petted me a lot, as they got into the car. But they wouldn't let me in. Where were they going, leaving me all alone?

I shouted and ran behind their car for a long distance but lost sight of it in the busy traffic. I came home crying and waited and waited for almost three days. But they never returned. Some new people came there and started cleaning up the place. They drove me out of the compound every time I went in. I felt very sad. I slept on the platform, ate whatever I could rummage in the dustbin, which I had hated all these years, and cursed myself for being a dog.

All my foes on the street rejoiced at my state. I could never fight with them as I had imagined, since I was not used to such a life. I lost weight. I now look so dirty and feel itchy always. What a life! How could my family leave me all alone, when they took all the others away with them?

Is it because I am a dog? How selfish these humans are! God let me always be born a dog and not as a selfish human being!

❑❑❑

3

Sweety's Resolution

"Sweety, please have your breakfast soon. Your school shuttle will be arriving anytime now," called out Mom.

Sweety took the small packet, opened it and gobbled the pill, i.e., her breakfast. Then her mom opened the locker in the kitchen and took out the precious little water bottle. She removed the filler and dropped a few drops of water into Sweety's mouth. "Sweety, wear your oxygen mask and anti-infra-red vest quickly."

Sweety felt irritated to wear these things. How nice and free she was inside her house! But nobody could go out without these. She went to the anteroom, wore the vest, the mask and the heavy boots. After wearing all that, she could not move around much. So, she sat near the door petting her robot Moron – a dog.

"Peem, peem." That was her school shuttle.

"Bye mom," she said and was off to the shuttle. Yes, it was a space shuttle specially designed to carry children to school. Sweety lived on Mars. Her school was on Earth. She got into the shuttle and greeted the pilot Mr Wilbert. All the children wore masks and vests like her. She sat and belted herself and the shuttle took off.

They were at the school in an hour. Sweety was desperate to get into the school building to remove all her extra fittings. She breathed a sigh of relief and went to her class. The classroom was full of computers, gadgets, headphones, chords and buttons. As soon as all the children sat in their places, the computers became active. Thus began their session. Today, Sweety had games and she loved games. She waited eagerly for the games period.

In the games period, they all went into that big room which had a variety of toys made from plastic, metal, cardboard and cloth. There were computers and electronic toys for older children. She played the computer game *Forest*. It always amused her because she could see a great variety of animals, birds and, above all, huge trees, on the screen. Her science teacher told them that all those things existed on Earth a few hundred years ago. She said that her great grandfather had seen all those things and recorded them in his diary. How lucky!

Her teacher also mentioned how her great grandfather had written that there existed huge water bodies (of fresh water) called rivers and lakes, which flowed into the oceans. People could drink as much water as they wanted, and they even bathed in water. Sweety was surprised how one could bathe in water. People now only swabbed their bodies with moist sponge brushes. It seems people could go out without these extra fittings and they could see trees all around them. They had real dogs and cats as pets in their homes. They ate a variety of food items called vegetables, cereals, fruit, meat, eggs, etc. They would prepare a wide range of dishes by cooking them on fire. How strange!

These days people ate only readymade pills of different sizes, colours and flavours. How could people cook food on fire?! Sweety was lost in her thoughts when her friend Sharon called her: "Sweety, it's time. Let's go. The shuttle will leave shortly."

Sweety quickly gathered her CDs and DVDs and ran to the front hall to wear her mask and vest. The shuttle took off and Sweety could see bright stars in the dark space outside the window.

As soon as she entered her house, Sweety quickly removed her mask and vest and called out, "Mom! Today, my science teacher told me some very interesting things. Come. I will tell you," and ran towards the kitchen.

She slipped and fell with a thud. "Oh Mom!" Sweety cried and woke up with a jolt.

"What happened Sweety? Did you have a nightmare?" her Mom stood by, caressing her hair.

Sweety's heart was beating loudly. She looked around the room. Then she rose and ran to the window. She saw sparrows and crows making noisy sounds and perching on the huge tree in their compound. The cool morning breeze soothed her. She saw Snoopy, her pet dog, happily playing with a ball in the garden. She quickly went to her bookshelf and felt all the books.

"Oh my! The dream was really dreadful Mom."

Her mother hugged Sweety, concerned. "You can relate your dream later. Brush your teeth and drink milk. Today I have prepared your favourite *parathas* for breakfast. Don't you have your test today?" her Mom asked.

Sweety sniffed the delicious aroma of *parathas* and felt so nice to see all things in their place. She recollected her science teacher's words: "The earth will not be the same, if we abuse nature like this. We have a limited supply of natural resources and have to save them for the future by using them wisely. We should not waste. The globe is warming up because of pollution, and one day the climate will change so much that we will not be able to walk outside without special outfits to save us from extreme cold or the infra-red rays of the sun. We will run out of pure oxygen and may require oxygen masks. So many species of animals and birds are becoming extinct and one day there may not be any creatures left on this earth. We need all kinds of lives for such comfortable living."

So, Sweety's dream was the result of this lecture! Thank God it was only a dream!

Sweety made up her mind to join the eco-protection group that the school had formed yesterday and work to protect the environment. Relieved, she ran out into the garden to breathe the fresh morning air and thank nature for all her gifts.

❑❑❑

4

The Mission

"Did you hear this news?" asked Sharu aunty and my ears immediately stood up, although I was supposed to be reading a novel, because Sharu aunty always had some juicy news!

"What is it?" asked my mom in a soft tone, intending not to disturb me or, rather, not wanting me to hear unwanted things.

"Narayan's son Deepak has run away," aunty answered in a hushed tone.

"Run away? What do you mean?" asked my mom with concern.

"It seems he failed his SSLC exams, so Narayan and Aarti gave him a piece of their mind two days ago. Since yesterday morning the boy is missing. They have lodged a police complaint. Somebody told them that Deepak was seen at Marenahalli, which is beyond those green hills. So, yesterday Narayan went to Marenahalli and looked for Deepak but failed to find him. Poor parents! They are so anxious. I tell you, children are really going beyond limits," aunty fumed.

Green hills. Those were the beautiful hills which we could see from our backyard. They were so named by the residents of our colony, as they looked green from the colony. I always wondered what was on those hills and beyond.

I stealthily ran to Mary's house. "Mary, did you know that Deepak has run away from home? People say he has gone to Marenahalli," I said, full of interest.

"Is that so? Where is Marenahalli? Why did he run away?" Mary asked me.

"Deepak failed in SSLC and his parents scolded him. That's why he has run away. I heard Sharu aunty tell my mom that Marenahalli is beyond those green hills. Shall we go and search for him?" I enquired.

"How can we go? The hills are so far away. Will our parents allow us to go?" she asked worriedly.

"We will form a group of around ten children and tell our parents that we are going on a trekking expedition to the green hills," I said.

"Trekking? Who will escort us?" she asked.

"We will request Raju Bhaiya to escort us. We have gone with him on so many treks and our parents will not object," I said.

"That's a good idea," said Mary.

In two days, we formed a group of 12, including Raju Bhaiya. Geetha, Lata, Suresh, Nawaz, Ganpat, Jitu, Meera, Suman, Shrikant, Binu, Jeevan, Mary and I, led by Raju Bhaiya, got ready for the expedition. Of course, we did not tell our parents about our intention of looking for Deepak. Since it was our vacation, they thought the expedition was for entertainment.

We packed our lunch and some fruits and eatables to be eaten on the way, and armed ourselves with water bottles, torches and raincoats. We put on our caps and set out early in the morning. Though our goal was to look for Deepak, when we left in a group, we were all thrilled and excited about the expedition. Those green hills were wooing us since long and though we had been on many treks to specific points, we had never before ventured forth into a trek like this with no specified point to reach.

We could see acres and acres of paddy fields belonging to the villagers nearby. Each of us carried a stick and backpack. We trekked in a row on the borders of the fields, singing our school chorus songs and popular film hits. Villagers working in the fields stopped their work for a while and looked at us in amusement.

As we walked, our excitement grew. The hills were getting nearer. We could clearly see the trees covering the hills with their green, and a small temple on top of one of the hills.

"Where is Marenahalli?" Raju Bhaiya asked a villager.

"Can you see that temple? Go there and you will see Marenahalli on the other side," replied the villager.

We reached the end of the fields just before noon. We crossed the big highway and on the other side stretched the forest area. Our hearts thumped as we entered the cool forest. Huge trees of all kinds created a big umbrella. On the ground were small, bushy, thorny plants. There were creepers and climbers everywhere. We could hear all sorts of sounds made by birds and insects.

We walked for an hour and all of us were tired. Spreading our mats under a huge *neem* tree, we opened our lunch-boxes. That was the best time we had during our trek! We eagerly looked at all the boxes. The aroma of delicious dishes wafted around.

"Wow! Vegetable *pullao*?" exclaimed Meera.

"Look at these delicious soft *parathas*," said Jeetu.

My mom had packed soft, white *idlis* and spicy *sambar*. She had also packed attractive coconut cakes. So we had many wonderful things to eat and ate to our hearts' content. Then we all sat back and relaxed.

After an hour, we set off again. Though the weather was hot, since we were in the forest area, we never felt the heat. The cool breeze soothed us. We ploughed through the bushes with the help of our sticks and began climbing the hill. Raju Bhaiya had a lot of experience and he led us along a *kutcha* pathway the villagers normally used. Nawaz and Suman entertained us with jokes and riddles. As we neared the temple, our excitement grew.

At last we reached the temple.

"Hey, we are here!" we all shouted with joy.

There were not many people there, as the temple was closed. We went around the temple and saw neat stone steps on the other side. Down below we could see houses like matchboxes and roads like snakes. The scene was breathtaking. We could hear film songs in the distance. We asked a passerby where Marenahalli was and he pointed to a beautiful place below.

We sat under a tree, ate fruits, drank water and relaxed. Then we began descending the steps. I prayed to God and vowed that if we found Deepak we would thank Him on our way back and continue our trek. Since going down the steps did not take much time, we reached Marenahalli by evening.

It was a cute little village with neat *kutcha* roads. Most houses were built of mud and had tiled or thatched roofs. It looked so different from our quarters. Cows, buffaloes, sheep and hens were all over the village. We walked through the narrow lanes, as village kids stared at us eagerly.

'Ramananda Ashram', a signboard declared. On seeing this board, Raju Bhaiya stood by and was lost in thought. The ashram was very beautiful and serene. We could see huge trees on both sides of the path leading from the gate to a bamboo structure. We entered the gate and were awestruck by a lovely garden between rows of trees. Flowers of all colours beckoned us. The tops of mango and guava trees were loaded with fruit and seemed so inviting. Though we were tempted to pluck them, we controlled ourselves and simply stepped into the lovely ashram built of neat bamboo sticks.

"Yes?" asked a young man in saffron.

"*Namaste!* We are from the colony beyond these hills and have just come on a trek. Could we meet Swamiji?"

"Welcome. Of course, you can meet him. Please come in."

The sadhu led us to a tranquil room where Swamiji sat on a bamboo mat, chanting mantras.

"Please sit down," said the young sadhu and all of us sat on the mat spread on the floor.

It was very silent and peaceful in there. The cool breeze made us feel as if the room had an air-conditioner. After a few minutes, Swamiji opened his eyes and smiled at us.

"Hello children. What brings you here?" he asked.

"Swamiji, we are from the colony on the other side of these hills. We were curious to see this side and so, we trekked this way. Your ashram is very beautiful, Swamiji. Recently, a boy named Deepak ran away from his home in our colony and we've heard he came here. So, we have come looking for him," Raju Bhaiya explained in detail.

Ran away from his home? Why would he come here? pondered Swamiji. "Anyway, it is already evening. You can relax and stay overnight. I will enquire about your friend. If God so wills, you will indeed find him," assured Swamiji.

All of us then discussed the situation in hushed tones. We had not informed our parents that we might be staying overnight. Now, how were we to inform them?

"What's the matter?" enquired Swamiji.

"Swamiji, we had told our parents we would return by evening. If we stay back, we need to inform them. Otherwise, they will be worried," I said.

"That's not a problem. Sadananda, please help these children make a call to their parents and then take them to the *Vishranthi Griha*. Also arrange for their dinner."

So, we called our parents and then stayed back in that serene place. A sumptuous dinner of a different kind was served. There were lots of fresh fruit as well as dry fruits as part of the dinner. Thereafter, we had nice, sound sleep and our tired bodies received perfect rest.

Early in the morning, a variety of birds began chirping and we woke up refreshed. We had a quick bath and were served hot breakfast and milk. Then we went to Sadananda Swami to find out if they could get any information.

"Veeraiah, who works for a small factory in Ramanathpura, told me that only a couple of days ago, a boy named Ramu had joined the canteen near his factory. He looked well fed and from a good family. Maybe you could try meeting Ramu," said Sadananda Swami.

We found out that Ramanathpura was just five kilometres away from the village. Raju Bhaiya said he would go along with Veeraiah on his bike and check up because we had little time. So the rest of us stayed back at the ashram. Our curiosity grew every moment and we prayed that Ramu would turn out to be Deepak.

Raju Bhaiya returned with Ramu two hours later. What a surprise! Ramu indeed turned out to be Deepak. He was so overwhelmed with emotion on seeing us all that tears automatically began rolling down his cheeks.

"I am sorry, Swamiji. I am Deepak and I ran away from home fearing that my parents would punish me for failing in the SSLC exams," said Deepak between sobs.

"But Deepak, your parents are so worried about you! Why would they punish you? If they scolded you for not putting in enough efforts, what's wrong? Isn't it their right? They want you to realise your responsibilities and study well for your own good," advised Swamiji gently.

"Yes Deepak. Your parents are very upset. They want to help you do whatever you are interested in. All our parents scold us when we waste time or neglect our responsibilities. But they do so only out of love for us. Who else will be so concerned about us?" I said.

"I am sorry. I want to go back home Swamiji. Please pardon me and bless me," Deepak said.

"Of course, son. God is with you. You shall prosper wherever you are. Obey and respect your parents and do your duty with devotion," said Swamiji.

We all hugged Deepak and took leave of the inmates in that lovely ashram.

"How did you escape your father's search when he came here two days ago?" I asked Deepak.

"I first went to Srinagar. But I soon realised that it is tough for a boy just to live there, because everybody started questioning me about my past. I set off from there and came here. I first went to the village chief's house because that was the biggest house and asked for a job. The chief got suspicious when I told him that I was an orphan. He said he would hand me over to the police, as some person had come looking for his son." Deepak was visibly losing control over himself as he continued.

"I begged him not to, telling him that I was not Deepak but Ramu from a village in north Karnataka and had lost my parents in an accident. But I knew he did not believe my story. I waited for a convenient opportunity and ran away from there to Ramanathpura. Of course, the canteen manager also doubted my story but gave me the job, saying he would make his own enquiries and till then I could work." Deepak now broke down, sobbing into his cupped palms.

"Now don't cry. Seek your parents' pardon and try to be a good boy in future," said Raju Bhaiya.

After lunch at the ashram, we set off for our colony. We climbed up the hill, went to the temple and offered our thanks. Then we climbed down the other side. The descent was very fast. It grew darker and Raju Bhaiya was getting worried. "Come on quick, quick," he kept saying.

The wonderful scene of the sunset woke up the artist in us. We captured the scene in our minds to make beautiful pictures when we returned home. Flocks of birds flew above us in various patterns, chirping merrily.

On reaching the highway around 7.15 pm Raju Bhaiya said, "We shall catch the bus from here, as it is already dark and we cannot walk through the fields in darkness."

Deepak sat next to me in the bus. He said he was very ashamed of having run away from home. He now realised the value of a protected home. He also realised how much his parents and little sister loved him and said he would never again do such a thing in life.

As soon as we got off the bus at our colony, we saw our parents waiting eagerly at the bus stop, since it was already 8 o'clock in the night. They were all worried about us. But the moment they saw Deepak with us, their joy knew no bounds. We all went in a group to Deepak's house and never in my life had I witnessed such an emotional scene.

Deepak's parents and sister hugged and kissed him and cried in joy. That's when I understood that joy also brought tears to our eyes. "Sorry Mom, sorry Dad," Deepak said between sobs.

But they would not let him speak further and said, "Deepu *beta*, forget everything. Let's begin afresh and first celebrate your homecoming."

"Thank you Raju and thank you children for bringing my son home safely. Next Sunday, we shall host a dinner for everybody at our house. Please don't fail to join us," said Deepak's father.

Thereby ended our most memorable trek, the memories of which shall linger in our minds forever.

❑❑❑

5

The Turning Point

Dear Mummyji,

I reached Delhi safely on the 19th. My journey was comfortable. Pappaji's friend Dev uncle had come to the station. He is a very nice man. I am very comfortable in his house. He has given an assurance that he will find a suitable room for me soon. I too have spoken to my colleagues.

By the way, I reported for duty on the 21st. The office is very posh and the people are very friendly. I found two guys from Bangalore. Right now I'm under training. The day I reported was an unforgettable one in my life. I had never imagined such a life in my childhood. It's all because of you that I am here today. I cannot ever forget what you have done for me, Mummyji.

Delhi is nice. But no city can match our Mysore! I miss that beautiful city, you, Pappaji, Vahini Behen and, of course, my dear Bhaiya Vivek, very much. Vivek Bhaiya is lucky to have found a job in Bangalore. He can meet you fairly often.

I have written to my home too. I'll write to Vivek Bhaiya. My sashtang namaskarams *to Pappaji. Take care of your health. Now that both Vivek Bhaiya and I have begun earning, please think of taking voluntary retirement and relax.*

With heaps of love and respect,

Yours fondly,

Kittu

Sandhya's eyes were moist by the time she finished reading this letter. Life was really very strange and thrilling. For a moment, she shuddered to think of what Kittu would have been today had she not taken an important decision 16 years ago! God is great in imparting sense to certain people's minds at the right time.

Sandhya had just reached home from office and there were umpteen things to finish yet. However, after reading this letter, she felt light and wanted to relive her past for a few minutes. She made herself a hot cup of coffee and sat on the swing in the verandah – her favourite spot.

****

Vivek was seven years old then. Sandhya had just been promoted as an officer in a nationalised bank. Her husband Balu was an executive in a multinational company. Sandhya had opted to travel to a nearby rural branch of her bank, which was 80 km away from Madras. It was just six months after she had reported at that branch that Sandhya conceived. Already, she had much planning to do at home with a seven-year-old son around. And now this second child! Sandhya was very worried. Vahini was born at Mysore, where Sandhya's parents lived. Sandhya kept worrying about her future.

"Don't worry so much, Sandhya. We'll see that we get some help for you when you go back. I have told several people. I'll help you for a month or two, or till such time as you are here," said Sandhya's mother.

Kittu, the son of Lakshmamma (the maid at Sandhya's mother's place), would come with his mother almost daily.

"Why, Lakshmamma! Doesn't he go to school? Why does he come with you everyday?" asked Sandhya.

"No, Didi, he doesn't go to school. I sent him to the government school for a year. He failed and got into bad company. His father is a drunkard and doesn't care for the family. I cannot afford putting Kittu in a better school. Nor do I have the time to keep a vigil on him." Lakshmamma looked enquiringly, then added, "Didi, why don't you take him with you to Madras? He'll help you at home and take care of the baby too. He's good at household work. He's already ten years old and if he's left alone at home, he'll become a rowdy."

That sounded a good idea to Sandhya. Lakshmamma was a very hardworking, sincere and honest lady. By taking Kittu, she would be helping Lakshmamma and also herself.

Vivek had become very friendly with Kittu in the two months that he spent at Mysore. He was thrilled when he heard Kittu was going to accompany them to Madras. He was already growing jealous of the new baby and wanted male company to tease her.

However, on reaching Madras, he was in for a shock. Kittu was not kept free to play with him. Sandhya made him work from dawn to dusk and, in her absence, he had to take care of that nag Vahini.

"Oh no! Amma, don't call Kittu, we're playing," Vivek would cry when his mother called Kittu to help her in the kitchen when she came home from the bank.

"Didn't I tell you in the morning to fold all the clothes? What were you doing the whole day?" she would shout.

Kittu shivered at her shouting and answered meekly, "Mummyji, Vahini did not let me do anything today. She cried all day. She has caught a cold, Mummyji."

"You always have a ready answer," snapped Sandhya. "Now come and wash these vessels fast. We are going to have guests for dinner and I have loads of things to do. Vivek! You better do your homework. Don't disturb Kittu. He is not here to play with you. He has come to work," she said sharply, venting her anger on Vivek.

Vivek was in Standard III when his teacher one day told them the story of *Great Expectations* and explained how, even to this day, children were exploited and made to work at an age when they should be playing and

attending school. Vivek immediately thought of Kittu. After all, Kittu was almost as young as he was. He was not sent to school but made to work from morning till night. From that day, Vivek began pitying Kittu.

On 14 November that year, the schoolchildren took out a rally against child labour. Vivek felt guilty, as in his own home a child was made to work.

He came home that day and told his mother: "Amma, today we went on a rally shouting slogans against child labour. Then I thought when I go to school, why should not Kittu also be sent to school? Why should he work, Amma? Doesn't his father earn?" asked Vivek innocently.

"No dear, his father is not earning enough. They cannot afford to send Kittu to school. They need his income too. There are many children like Kittu. How can we solve everybody's problem?" Sandhya answered.

"Amma, true we cannot solve everybody's problem. But are you and Daddy not earning enough to send Kittu to my school? He is clever Amma. The other day I taught him the alphabet and numbers and he writes so well. It seems he loves to study. Please send him to my school, Amma," said Vivek.

That night, Sandhya could not sleep. She felt ashamed that despite being educated and well-informed, she had made another's child work for her for almost a year, whereas her little child had understood how wrong that was. In her selfishness, she had not given a thought to this issue.

After much thinking, she came to a decision. "Balu, Balu," she woke her husband up.

"What's wrong? Are you not feeling sleepy? Don't you have to go to office tomorrow? Then sleep!" he grumbled.

"Balu, lost in our selfish world, we have committed a blunder! We have made a child work for us an entire year: a child almost as old as our Vivek, whom we pamper and dote upon. Vivek as a child has realised this and we as adults did not. I feel guilty, Balu. I have decided one thing. We'll put Kittu in school and educate him. He is a bright boy," Sandhya said.

"Don't be silly, Sandhya. What will you do with Vahini? You and your mother were the ones who got this bright idea and now you talk like this! After all, we are paying Kittu's parents well and that's what they now need most. Kittu is not the only child working. There are millions of children toiling for their families. At least Kittu is being looked after well. We cannot solve the problems of society. Forget your guilt and sleep now," Balu snapped.

However, Sandhya could not ignore the issue so easily. Kittu's pathetic face kept haunting her, as she was a mother. How could she have been so stone-hearted all this time?

The next day, she convinced Balu and looked out for a babycare centre for Vahini nearby. She availed of a week's leave, ran around and got Kittu admitted in a nearby school. Kittu was surprised by the entire turn of events.

"Mummyji, if my parents come to know, they'll beat me. They sent me here to work for you," Kittu said.

"Kittu, don't get scared. I'll convince your parents. I'll help them financially too. From today, you are not a servant here. You are like Vivek, my son. Your duty now is to study well and prove yourself. Only then will all my efforts be fruitful," Sandhya replied.

Kittu was too thrilled by the sudden boon. He decided to make use of the opportunity well. He was full of gratitude for Sandhya. Even at that tender age, he had the maturity to understand that Sandhya's act was very noble, and though he did go to school, he assisted Sandhya in his free time.

Gradually, he earned the love and affection of one and all in the family. He felt more at home with this family than in his real home, which he visited during holidays. He felt sad to see his brother Putta toil in an auto garage and his sister Manju do the same in a garment factory. How lucky he was to have found a goddess!

Just this year, Kittu had completed his B.Com (Hons.) and was hired by a multinational finance company in Delhi after a campus interview. Balu and Sandhya were in Mysore for the last five years and that is where Kittu did his course. By now, Kittu was like their own son.

The day they saw him off at the Railway Station was a memorable one. Sandhya choked with emotion and Vahini cried openly. Vivek and Balu hid their feelings by cracking silly jokes. Kittu's brother and mother too had come to the station. They were in tears and could not believe that Kittu was from their family. They fell at Balu's feet, thanking and praising him profusely.

****

"Sandhya, what is this? The door is wide open and you're in your own world. Why are you crying? Whose letter is that? Where is Vahini?" Balu kept shooting question after question.

Sandhya silently handed over the letter to Balu and waited for him to read it.

Then she spoke with rare confidence: "Who said we cannot change the world as individuals, Balu? Each of us can do wonders. Just imagine, if we had continued to treat Kittu as a servant, what would he have been today? Don't you feel proud and satisfied that you successfully changed the course of one good soul? If more people realise their responsibilities and capabilities like we have, it will be more than enough to make this world a wonderful place to live in."

"Yes darling, I agree. By changing our attitude towards Kittu, not only did Kittu benefit but we have also gained. We have secured a loving son," Balu answered and quickly turned away to hide his welling tears.

❑❑❑

6

The Red Monster

When I look at certain plants, I am reminded of the scents of their flowers and the taste of their fruits. You won't believe it, but my mouth starts producing saliva when I smell tasty fruits and food items or even if I think of them. This may happen to any of you sometimes in life.

Besides, certain smells remind me of certain places and people. For example, whenever I smell delicious *rasam*, I think of my grandma; whenever I smell fresh *idlis*, I associate it with a city I used to visit often during my childhood, where fresh *idlis* were sold on the street during the early morning hours. And the scent of jasmine flowers reminds me of the temple town I visited about 20 years ago, where I was intoxicated with the lovely scent of jasmine as I walked down the narrow lane to the temple, for both the sides were occupied by flower sellers.

Whenever I receive a letter by post, which rarely happens these days thanks to e-mail, I am reminded of Ramaiah Maama!

My childhood is highlighted by certain memories and those of Ramaiah Maama also come under this category. The innocent residents of Kattorapuram (a town on the edge of the forest) can never forget Ramaiah Maama. Daily they would wait eagerly for him. He not only delivered letters but did a lot more. He would read and write letters for people, sell stamps, pass on oral messages, educate people about various postal services, make general enquiries and also be present on all happy and sad occasions in the village.

Ramaiah lived all alone on Agrahara Lane, in a single-room tenement rented out to him by the village chief. I do not know anything about his family or the reason why he lived all alone. As a child, I never bothered to find out these things.

After delivering letters to the 50-odd houses in our village, Ramaiah Maama would set off for the forest on his cycle, happily singing or whistling tunes of old film hits.

"Maama, why do you go into the forest everyday?" we children asked him one day.

"I go to deliver letters to people in Vanarajapuram, children."

"Vanarajapuram? Do people live inside forests?"

"Vanarajapuram is on the other side of the forest and this is the only route to reach there."

"Aren't there wild animals in the forest? Aren't you scared to enter the forest? How about people in Vanarajapuram? Aren't they scared of wild animals?"

"Children, the people there are tribals who have been living in forests since birth. They depend on forests for their living. They are not scared. In fact, they befriend animals."

"How far is Vanarajapuram?"

"About 15 kilometres away."

"Fifteen kilometres through this thick jungle, oh my! Don't they have a postman?"

"No children. I am the Runner* for that village and I have to do my duty. I am not scared of animals. They are my friends."

"Runner? What does that mean? Do you run?" chuckled one of us.

"Yes, children. I actually used to run through the forests. Like me there are many others who are runners serving the remote villages. Thanks to your parents, I was gifted this bicycle a few years ago and now I cycle, though my post is that of a Runner."

"But when you run through the jungle daily, don't the wild animals worry you?" I persisted.

---

* *There existed a post called 'Runner' in the postal department during the British Raj. Runners were appointed to deliver letters to certain areas not well connected with roads, by literally running. This story is based on a real-life incident.*

"No! No! As I said, they are my friends."

"Friends!"

Now, that was a very interesting thing for us. Except cattle, dogs and cats, we could never imagine any other animal being friendly with human beings. Every evening when Ramaiah Maama returned from the forest, we would run to receive him, because on many days he would bring us certain rare flowers, fruits and nuts. He would find joy in distributing these to as many children as possible.

I still remember how during the rainy season Ramaiah Maama came in drenched from the heavy rain. His flimsy raincoat hardly served the purpose. Even then, he would not forget to get us our share of fruits or nuts. He would go straight home, change his clothes and then call us.

Everybody in the village loved Ramaiah Maama and he was welcomed by one and all. He would be offered coffee or tea and snacks by many people, but rarely did he accept the offer. He preferred cooking for himself. I sometimes watched him do kitchen work very meticulously. His kitchen, which was just a corner of the single room he occupied, looked so neat and clean.

When I told my mother this and said her kitchen was no match for his, she was mad and said, "*Arrey*, what great things will a bachelor cook? After all, he feeds only himself and may manage only with *rasam* and rice. But here I have to feed a family of eight. Each one wants the items he likes most and there's none to help me. How can you be so insensitive and compare me with that man?"

On Sunday evenings, Ramaiah Maama would sit under the *peepal* tree, on the neat cement platform built around its trunk and relate interesting stories and anecdotes to the assembled children. We would all eagerly wait for those sessions, as there was no television or cinema to entertain us in our village.

"Last week, as I was coming through the forest, I saw our friend Jumbo the elephant crying. Yes, I peeped into the pit near where she stood crying and was shocked to see her baby had fallen into the pit. The mother elephant would try to extend her trunk but could not reach the baby. The baby was badly hurt and moaning. I felt miserable. But I was scared to go too close. I came here and called up the forest officer, Sharmaji. He sent a team of people with equipment and they lifted the baby out. Thankfully, the baby was alive and I felt good."

We all gaped at Ramaiah Maama in awe. He then continued: "Children, today I saw a beautiful peacock in the forest. He spread his lovely feathers wide and danced. It was such a marvellous scene. I did not feel like coming back."

The next day he would say: "I was surprised when a lovely little blackbird responded to my whistles yesterday. Every time I whistled, he would coo. It was fun."

And on the next... "Today it is hot. I am sure the tigers will come to drink water at the pond in the afternoon. Last time, I saw about seven or eight of them at the pond. Handsome and healthy tigers with shining orange coats! By the way, can any of you tell me whether the tiger is orange in colour with black stripes or black in colour with orange stripes?"

We were confused. How could Ramaiah Maama be so cool and brave after seeing tigers so closely!

Thus, as the days passed we realised Ramaiah Maama was well versed with animal life and could even converse with some animals and birds! He knew how they lived and where they would be during different seasons. He knew when they were angry or hungry or happy. He knew which animals were friendly and which were dangerous. He enjoyed the company of animals more than he enjoyed human company.

He would joyfully enter the forest with his mailbag. And would then tell us about tribal life on the other side. Many a time he would run errands for those people, carrying small things they required from our village. He once even got us small toys that they made from roots and wood.

****

I still remember that miserable day when the big red mail van arrived in our village. Ramaiah Maama looked worried. A team of people came and spoke to our elders and inspected the edge of the forest. They spoke for a long time and patted Ramaiah Maama's back.

"You need not struggle anymore, Ramaiah. You can take care of the small office here and earn your living. You need not go into that dangerous forest. They are going to clear it and lay a road so that our mail van can deliver the letters to the other village," said the officer in a black coat.

"But Sir, I don't consider this a struggle. In fact, I enjoy my work. I love this forest. Why fell trees to lay a road? I can take care of this job," replied Maama anxiously.

"No, Ramaiah. We are not the ones to decide. The plans are made by higher-ups. We only implement them. They have removed the post of Runner," was the reply.

Thereafter, the work was carried out quite swiftly. A *kutcha* road was laid through the forest, felling hundreds of huge trees. Ramaiah Maama was never as cheerful as before. As each tree fell with a loud thud, Maama almost cried. He would close his ears to the cruel sounds of the axe. He continued to deliver letters riding along the new road for some time until the mail van arrived. But he had changed a lot. He wore a sorry look. He no more told us stories. Neither did he get us anything from the forest. He would get into his room immediately on arrival and shut the door. Even when we wished him, he responded half-heartedly with a lost look.

****

That day was the first day the mail van was to enter the forest. The driver picked up his mailbag and got into the van. Just then, Ramaiah Maama suddenly emerged from the small office room, stood across the van and shouted. "You tell me that I should not go into this forest? *Arrey*, this is my forest and those animals are my friends. How can you take away my work? Get off you idiot!"

The driver was stunned and all the people around were shocked to witness Maama's behaviour. Tears were rolling down his cheeks. My father and the others pacified Maama. "This is a natural development. Changes have to take place. The post of Runner has been abolished. You cannot stop it, Ramaiah. Why get so disturbed? After all, you have your job. Take things as they come."

Thereafter, Maama's condition only worsened gradually. He could not control his feelings. Everyday, he created scenes, abusing the driver and pelting stones at the van. He would not take care of his work in the office.

****

Within a year, complaints were lodged and a new postmaster arrived. Ramaiah Maama lost his job. He took to drinking. Every morning, he drank and entered the forest talking to himself. His clothes were always dirty and tattered. He no more cooked or maintained the house. But out of compassion, the landlord did not throw him out. People of the village fed him whenever he came begging, because they could not forget the old Ramaiah.

Ramaiah Maama had nothing in his life other than delivering letters, communicating with animals and birds and talking to little children. The monster mail van had taken away all his pleasures and he could not bear it. I was in that village till my tenth standard and, thereafter, I went to the nearby town for further studies. I stayed in a hostel and visited my village during holidays. Every time I went there, I would see Maama, wish him and sit with him, though he no more recognised individuals or spoke sense. But he would sit peacefully when somebody spoke softly to him and just gaze at the trees.

Once during my visit, Ramaiah Maama was not to be seen. I asked my mother about him and she said he had gone missing since the previous day. I was worried. In the afternoon, after lunch, I set out into the forest along with a group of friends. The forest was no more wild and dense, as buses, vans and cycles sped through it. Many trees had been felled and we could see large tracts of clear land.

About two kilometres inside, we heard some dry leaves rustle and stopped. We looked around and were stunned to see the scene. Ramaiah Maama lay unconscious on the ground and a few elephants stood by him, just waving their trunks. We were scared to go nearby.

We stood helplessly at a distance and you won't believe what we saw next. One of the elephants lifted Maama gently in her trunk and began walking towards the road. The other elephants walked back into the forest. We quickly hid on the other side of the road and watched. The elephant slowly walked to the road, stopped, turned towards the village and resumed walking. We followed the elephant at a distance. After about two furlongs, the elephant placed Maama gently on the road and got back into the forest.

We stood motionless for a few minutes and then went near him, as we heard the sound of an approaching bus. We carried him to one side and found that he was not hurt. We had a water bottle and splashed some water on his face. He opened his eyes slowly. By then the bus had come near and the driver stopped to see what had happened.

We took Ramaiah Maama to the local doctor, who said that he must have fainted from exhaustion and hunger. Nothing was wrong with him. I took Maama home and served him a good dinner. He ate hurriedly. Tears rolled down my cheeks. What a sorry state!

I was touched by the concern of the elephants for Maama. Till then I had only heard that animals were very friendly if we were good to them, but that day I had a live experience.

****

Four years passed by. In the meantime, I had completed my degree course and secured a job in Delhi. I went to my village after a six-month stint in Delhi and, as usual, decided to visit Maama. He was nowhere to be found. I asked my mother: "Amma, where is Ramaiah Maama? Has he gone into the forest again?"

"Kanna, I did not want to shock you as soon as you arrived. Ramaiah Maama is no more," my mother replied sadly.

I was shocked. "What happened?"

"That's a very sad story, Kanna. It seems like a fantasy but it happened right before our eyes. Two weeks ago, Ramaiah Maama was sitting near Ganesha's hotel. The mail van came into the village at the usual time, that is, around 11 o'clock. The driver went into the office to sort and pick up the mailbag. Ramaiah Maama had quietly moved towards the van and sat near one of the wheels on the other side. Nobody had observed this. Or those who saw him thought he would automatically get up when the van started. The driver got into the van and started it, without realising that Ramaiah was in front of the wheel. Ramaiah, who must have been resting against the wheel at that time, was suddenly pushed down. The van ran over him.

"The driver stopped immediately on feeling a thud, but it was too late. It was not his fault. But he cried a lot. 'What a sorry fate! Should the same van, which turned you mad, kill you? Ramaiah, please forgive me. I did not see you. Why did you have to sit there?' he wailed. Oh, the scene was heart-rending!"

Amma was overcome with emotion: "Will anybody believe this? That day you saw Ramaiah being helped and saved by an elephant, and here we saw him being mauled by a mechanical monster invented by man!"

I couldn't say a word. This was indeed an irony. When I narrate this story to my children today, they do not believe me and think I am adding spice to events and imagining too much. But I was a witness and will forever be reminded of my dear Ramaiah Maama and his tragic end, whenever I receive a letter!

❑❑❑

7

The Oath

Kamala was very excited. Her only son Mohan, a non-resident Indian settled in the Eden on earth – the United States of America – was coming on a month's vacation along with his wife Prema and children Satish and Anju, after three years. Her eyes and her heart were longing for this reunion. Of course, development in telecommunications had enabled her to speak to her son and his family over phone almost every week. But physical nearness is something no technology can match. Her longing to see, feel and hug her son would be fulfilled today.

Kamala was busy cooking a five-course meal of sweets and savouries prepared after elaborate soaking, grinding, frying, baking, pounding and what not! She had prepared Mohan's favourite sweet *kayi obbattu* a day before, as it involved a very laborious procedure. Her brown cotton saree contained samples of all the dishes she had cooked! White patches of flour, sticky spots of jaggery and black stains of oil adorned the saree.

"Amma, what is this? Mohan will be here in another hour. Go look at yourself in a mirror. You look horrifying. Please have a wash and get ready, Amma!" ordered her 28-year-old daughter Sarojini.

Sarojini lived in the same city of Bangalore in a well-planned extension area. Her husband Manoj, daughter Shubha and father Subba Rao had gone to the airport to fetch Mohan and his family. She had come to her mother's place the previous night and was excitedly looking forward to meeting her brother.

Kamala hurriedly finished cooking, cleaned the kitchen and went into the bathroom for a wash. The dim light in the bathroom did not hide the cobwebs hanging from the tiled roof of the bathroom. Kamala shouted from inside: "Kempa, hadn't I told you to clean the bathroom properly yesterday itself? Look at the ceiling. Cobwebs are hanging all over. Satish and Anju will get scared to bathe here. As soon as I come out, clear the cobwebs and spray that phenol Saro has brought."

"Sorry Amma, I forgot about the cobwebs. Yes, I will clear them immediately after you come out," answered Kempa, the only help Kamala and Subba Rao had.

Kempa came into their lives as a boy of ten and stayed back ever since. He knew all about the family and served them with utmost devotion. Subba Rao tried his best to coax him to join a school but Kempa showed no interest in studies. He preferred to do physical work and did not want to leave the family. He did not even want to marry. He considered Subba Rao's children and grandchildren his own and loved them dearly. The children too enjoyed Kempa's company very much.

"This gentleman will never change. Why can't he agree to renovate and redesign the house with Mohan's money? After all, this house only belongs to Mohan. How long can one suffer in this dust? I am fed up of cleaning this house," muttered Kamala to herself.

Subba Rao, the hero of our story, was 80 years old. Lean, lanky and bespectacled, he was the most active member of the family. Always dressed in white khadi dhoti and kurta, he was fondly called *chikka Gandhi Thatha* by everybody in the locality. He was a freedom fighter and typical Gandhian.

The present generation, which has only read about Gandhi in history, could comprehend to some extent why Gandhi was worshipped all over, by looking at Subba Rao! Right from naming his children after Gandhi and Sarojini Naidu and wearing only khadi clothes to resisting corruption, leading a very simple life and facing the anger of his family members and, above all, not supporting his son when he wished to go to the US, in practically everything, Subba Rao stuck to his Gandhian principles. That is why he even refused to receive the government pension for freedom fighters, saying that he did not fight for freedom seeking any personal benefit. That was his duty as a son of the soil. He worked as a teacher in a local school and brought up his children on the meagre income from that source.

Subba Rao was shocked when his son was adamant about going to the US for further studies. "Mohan, you have scored so well. You will get a good job here, or easily secure admission in the best institution. Why do you want to go there?"

"Appa, you do not understand. Getting admission in a US University with scholarship is so tough. I have got it and you are not allowing me to go. The infrastructure and the opportunities there are too good. I will study and return to India. Don't worry," said Mohan.

"If all young people fly away like this, how will your motherland prosper?" asked Subba Rao.

"I promise that I will definitely come back and serve India. Why do you doubt me?" replied Mohan in irritation.

Subba Rao knew for sure that he would not return, because he had seen scores of youngsters making false promises to parents and settling in the US for good. But at 65, he did not have any strength left to fight with his grown son. So he had to yield to his wishes. Kamala too supported Mohan. Thus flew the bird crossing the big oceans, something not acceptable to orthodox Hindus of those times.

As Subba Rao had feared, Mohan never ever thought of returning to India. Conveniently, he made America his home. In fact, this was the main attraction for Prema when Mohan entered the marriage market. Prema, a highly qualified doctor, readily accepted the proposal and flew to her new paradise. *Here flies the second bird!* thought Subba Rao. Then began the process of applying for various visas and cards.

"Amma, we have already received the green card," announced Mohan happily over the phone one night.

"What does that mean Mohan?" asked Kamala innocently.

"That means your son is solidifying his stay in America," replied Subba Rao in an acid tone. He had overheard the conversation on the speaker.

****

That was four years ago. Of course, Subba Rao was happy that his son and grandchildren were coming. But he was not as excited as Kamala, since he had developed a detachment towards all relationships. His only attachment was towards this soil, which was being exploited right and left after Independence. His heart ached when he remembered the tortures and insults that freedom fighters underwent at the hands of foreign rulers. How sad that our own countrymen do not even want to live here and serve the country... after all that struggle! What is wrong with the younger generation?

"Amma, they have come," shouted Sarojini excitedly and ran to open the main door.

Kamala came running. Her whole body trembled and her eyes automatically began shedding tears.

"Don't get so excited, Kamala. Your BP will shoot up," warned Subba Rao.

"Amma," said Mohan and hugged her tightly. His eyes were wet too. He then touched his father's feet.

Subba Rao took Mohan in his arms and patted his shoulders. "Welcome son... to this golden soil – your motherland," he said emotionally.

Satish and Anju were very excited to see their grandparents after so long. "Thatha, Ajji, do you know we have come to take you along with us?" they said.

"What? Take us along! Where to? We are happy where we are," said Subba Rao.

"Yes, Maava. The children are right. We are taking you along with us. Though your passports were ready for the last five years, you never made up your mind to visit us. This time, we have decided to take you along with us for a special occasion. You must not reject our invitation," said Prema.

"What is it Mohan? What is she saying?" asked Subba Rao with fear in his eyes.

"Come on Prema. Why are you raking up the subject immediately on reaching? I will tell them later. Now, let us all have our lunch. I am very hungry and tired," replied Mohan.

Green banana leaves were spread on the cement kitchen floor and narrow long bamboo mats were laid out beside them for the people to sit. Satish and Anju sat on them uncomfortably and looked queerly at their grandpa who squatted crossed legged with ease. They were not used to eating with their hands and struggled to eat the gravy items. Though Kamala had been very careful to ensure that the dishes were not too hot, since the kids were not used to spicy food, Satish and Anju could not relish even the bland food. Kamala was disappointed that they did not eat properly. However, they enjoyed the sweets. Subba Rao felt sad that the children were not even brought up as normal Indian kids. But he made no comment and had his lunch silently.

Mohan looked around the kitchen and saw that absolutely nothing had changed here since his last visit – why, since his childhood – except that an electric mixer now adorned the shelf. He remembered how he had to fight for days to convince his mother to use the mixer that he bought for her ten years ago. Of course, she resisted every change in this manner. The switch-over from firewood to gas stove was also quite tough. He saw the same shining yellow brass and bronze vessels, iron pans, iron cutter, etc. His thoughts went back to his college days...

Mohan would walk home from his college, which was around two kilometres away. His mother would be eagerly awaiting him at the door to serve him a hot meal in his round stainless steel plate in the kitchen. He loved to sit there under the high-tiled roof.

His mother's clothes hung neatly on the clothesline along the wall, shining dry vessels were stacked neatly on the shelf, small lamps were lit before pictures of gods and goddesses in one corner, white *rangoli* patterns adorned the floor in front of the gods, the lovely aroma of incense sticks, the smell of delicacies his mother served... were all unforgettable. Each vessel reminded him of a special dish: the lead vessel reminded him of the aromatic *rasam*, the heavy bronze one reminded him of delicious sweet *payasam*, the flat iron pan of crisp rice *rotis* and *kayi obbattus* and the deep pan of spicy *vadas.*

The kitchen had just two small windows and the curry-leave and *parijatha* trees could be seen through them. It was strange that the kitchen was cool in summers and warm in winters. Above all, the kitchen was the abode of his dear mother and her love filled the air all around.

****

Subba Rao and Kamala were thoroughly enjoying the company of Mohan and his family. Four or five days after their arrival, they were all sitting in the backyard, enjoying the milky moonlight and the aroma of white jasmines, *parijatha,* night queen and other flowers of the small garden that Kamala had grown.

"Appa, this time you must come with us to the US. Please don't make excuses. We are all getting citizenship and I would like you to attend the ceremony, which will be celebrated in a grand manner," said Mohan cautiously.

Subba Rao was taken aback. Citizenship! So his son has decided to transplant himself with his roots to an alien land! What irony! The son of a freedom fighter – who fought to drive foreigners out of the motherland – happily announcing his success in gaining acceptance as the citizen of a foreign country!

In fact, Subba Rao had been adamant that Kamala should not go to the US to help Prema when Anju was born, because he detested the whole idea of his son insisting that Anju should be born in the US to gain the many benefits later in life that were due to a natural citizen.

Prema's mother was sick and requested Kamala to go but Subba Rao sternly said: "Why cannot Prema come over here? If she is so particular of begetting her child there, she can as well manage herself."

Mohan was very upset for some time at his father's stubborn attitude but later realised how hurt he was by the changed outlook of his son, which was perhaps inevitable in today's world. "Appa, I understand your feelings. But I cannot help it. We both are in very good positions there and the children are getting the best of education and will have a whole lot of opportunities in the future. You come and stay with us here. You will have all comforts. Now there is nothing wrong going out in search of greener pastures, Appa. The world is shrinking and differences between countries are thinning out and exist only for political reasons," said Mohan.

"Mohan, if you are comfortable there, stay there. But please don't justify that. You may call me a fool but I will not accept your argument. I cannot come and stay there. That's for sure. But since you have been inviting us for long, we will just visit you, attend the ceremony and return. Please do not force us to stay back," said Subba Rao emphatically.

Kamala, who was looking at her husband hopefully, felt slightly relieved. Though she had no qualms about going to her son's house, she could not go all these years because of her total devotion to Subba Rao. She felt elated but did not show her joy, lest her husband read between the lines and cancel the trip.

****

After their first-ever air travel, Subba Rao and Kamala landed in the US with their son's family. Satish and Anju were thrilled at the thought of having their grandparents with them for a long time. They could leisurely spend more time with them than they did when they visited India, because there they were travelling or meeting relatives most of the time.

Subba Rao now told them stories of the freedom struggle and narrated incidents from the great Mahatma's life. They were awestruck that a human being could be so truthful and so devoted to social causes. Kamala entertained them with folk stories and taught them certain indoor games like *choukabara*, *kallata* (simple games played with just five or seven round stones), and many more. The only irritants Subba Rao could not adjust to were the English toilets and the absence of Kannada newspapers and, of course, he missed his dear motherland.

Mohan and Prema took every care to make them as comfortable as possible. They inwardly hoped that after some time, Subba Rao could be convinced to stay back, as he had started enjoying his grandchildren's company.

****

D-Day arrived. Mohan, Prema and the children dressed in their best outfits and Kamala wore Prema's Mysore silk saree for the first time. She had never worn silks after her wedding because Subba Rao would not allow her to do so. She could wear only cottons. Subba Rao was stunned to see Kamala in silk. She did indeed look beautiful. *Poor lady, she had to sacrifice a lot for my sake*, he thought.

"Prema forced me to wear this. I will wear it only today. Don't scold me," said Kamala fearfully.

Subba Rao chuckled and walked off silently. But Prema could not convince him to change over to silk. As usual, he wore his white khadi kurta.

Mohan and Prema were nervous. There were quite a few people waiting to be administered the oath of citizenship. "Mr Mohan, son of Mr Subba Rao, India," went the announcement.

Mohan went up to the stage and all eyes were on him. The gentleman administering the oath began reading, "I, Mohan, son of Subba Rao of India, hereby declare that...." Mohan kept repeating whatever he was asked to. Subba Rao's ears reddened on hearing words to the effect: "I pledge my allegiance to the United States of America and promise to fight for this country and use arms in case of war even against the country of my origin, i.e., India...."

Suddenly, Subba Rao began hearing: "*Vande Mataram, Vande Mataram, Bharat Chodo.* Quit India!" Scenes of the freedom processions in which he had participated, the merciless lathi beatings, the stunning sound of police firing, the painful cries of young marchers and the death of his dear friends Das and Ponnaiah began coming to his mind. He was just physically present here. On stage, he did not register the US officer reading the oath or his son Mohan repeating it. He saw the Mahatma orating emotionally and hundreds and thousands of *satyagrahis* listening to him with rapt attention.

Suddenly he felt a strong *lathi* hitting his chest. He held his chest and cried aloud in pain: "Amma!"

Kamala, who was intently watching the proceedings on stage, was shocked and turned towards Subba Rao. She immediately knew something was wrong and asked him in a low voice: "What's wrong? Are you alright?"

Her eyes were already filled with tears of sorrow and shock. All the neighbours rushed to help. "No, Kamala, I do not want to die here. Please save me and take me back to my homeland. Kamala, please take me away immediately," Subba Rao said between painful cries.

"What's he saying? Please call an ambulance," said one gentleman.

The whole place turned into an accident spot. The proceedings on stage were halted. Mohan came running and was shocked to see his father lying on his mother's lap. "Appa! What's wrong? Are you alright?"

Subba Rao was not alive to reply to his son – now an American citizen. His last words were, "*Vande Mataram*." He thanked his stars before dying that he did not hear his son repeating those humiliating words that the American officer had read out. But he was sad that he could not breathe his last in his motherland.

Little did Mohan or anyone there – except Kamala – realise the true cause of Subba Rao's sudden demise.

Glossary

Appa:	Father
Amma:	Mother
Maava:	Father-in-law
Kayi Obbattu:	A kind of sweet bread made out of wheat flour with filling of jaggery and grated coconut
Rasam:	Diluted spicy gravy side dish to be consumed with cooked rice
Vada:	Spicy eatable made of flour and pepper deep fried
Payasam:	Gravy-like sweet dish
Parijatha:	Beautiful white flower with red stalks and good scent used specially in worship
Bharat Chodo:	Quit India
Khadi:	Handwoven cotton cloth
Lathi:	Wooden stick used by the police
Ajji:	Grandmother
Thatha:	Grandfather
Jaggery:	Form of sugar extracted from sugarcane
Chowkabara:	Game played with dice
Kannada:	Language spoken in Karnataka

❑❑❑

8

The Interesting Chat

Razia was late. She had said she'd come by 7 o'clock. It was 7.45 and there was still no sign of her. Mehmood was tired after a busy day. He had worked from seven in the morning. Today, he had also performed two surgeries. Sipping hot coffee, he was lazily tapping the keyboard of his computer. He had got into the chat room for the first time just to see what it was like. He would get annoyed when his 16-year-old daughter spent hours chatting on the Internet. "How can you chat with strangers for so long, Razi? It's crazy. Why don't you do something more constructive?" he would shout.

"Daddy, you do not know the fun in this game. Just try it once and you will realise it. I have made so many new friends and I get so much information," she would reply.

****

So, let me see what this is all about, thought Mehmood and was going through numerous chat conversations, when one particular message made him pause and ponder.

It strengthens the bond
It lets it grow
It stays green forever
It penetrates all walls
Of colour, creed, caste, religion and nationality
It is the only saviour
To keep this beautiful world in one piece
Each one of us enjoys its bliss
Yet in groups we let it die
When will people warring with others realise
That only love and not hate will help them win?
Join me to spread the flavour of love
All over this wonderful world!

Mehmood liked the piece very much and read it again and again. He was tempted to reply and commented: 'That's a marvellous verse. I am curious to know your identity and join your club.'

Within seconds, he received a reply: 'Thank you for joining me. You are the 117th member of my club. For the present just know that my name begins with T. Call me T. Unless I get your identity, I will not reveal mine.'

'Okay, call me M. I am a surgeon.'

'I am an architect. Your sex and age, please.'

'I am a middle-aged male. How about you?'

'I am a middle-aged female. Married?'

'Yes. Father of a 16-year-old daughter. You?'

'Married. Mother of a 19-year-old son and 12-year-old daughter. Wife?'

'Was a very dynamic and lively teacher. Died of cancer two years ago.'

'I am sorry. Truly sorry. My husband is a professor of Physics in the local university. By the way, where do you live?'

'I live in San Francisco, US. Where do you live?'

'I am from Pune, India. Have you seen India?'

'Oh, of course. I am basically from India.'

'That's interesting. Where are you from?'

'That's interesting but very sad. I am from Bombay, which is now Mumbai.'

'Sad? What do you mean?'

"Daddy, sorry I'm late! Let's go!" Razia entered with a bang.

Mehmood suddenly realised where he was and quickly typed his last message: 'I have to leave. The rest some other time, Miss T. Bye,' and shut down the computer.

Razia peeped and exclaimed: "Daddy, you were chatting. That's wonderful! Whom were you chatting with?"

"I don't know. She is a lady from India. Seems an interesting personality," replied Mehmood.

"Didn't I tell you – chatting is fun!" Razia beamed.

"Yes, chatting is fun, Razi. How was your party? Were all your friends there?"

"The party was good. Except Donald and Radha, all of them were there. We are sad that next year most of us will be going to different places, Daddy. We were a close group. I will miss all of them, especially Ronald and Meher." Razia was almost in tears.

"Razi Beta, that's life. We thought we would never be able to live without your mom. Are we not living? Time is the best healer. You will get new friends who will help you bury your old memories without hurting yourself. Your mom helped me overcome my childhood pains. You are helping me overcome the pain of her loss. Thus the cycle goes on," said Mehmood.

That day's chat session lingered in Mehmood's mind. He had to continue. He was busy for the next whole week. On Sunday, Razia went to see her aunt at San Jose and Mehmood was free after the weekend cleaning job. He hurried to the computer and logged on to the chat session. Ms T was not there. However, he had noted her

e-mail ID the last time and so, he sent a mail, 'Ms T, I got back to continue our conversation. But couldn't get you. How are you?'

****

On Monday night, Mehmood received a reply, 'Mr M, Hi! How are you? I was away on work for a week. By the way, I am still curious about your background. Let's chat on Thursday at....'

The whole of Thursday Mehmood was excited and after Razia went to bed, he logged on to the chat room. There she was – Ms T. 'Ms T, I will tell you about my background. But first, you. Do you have any specific intention in chatting or is it just for fun?'

'That's a crazy question. People chat just for fun. You know it. Did you have anything particular in mind?'

'Of course not! But then your verse on love made me ask you so.'

'Oh that! You are intelligent, Mr M! Yes. I do have an intention. I want to spread love and stop wars.'

'That's funny. How can you stop wars by chatting with people?'

'That's not funny, Mr M. I have seen from close quarters how a small flicker of hatred can cause big wars. Thus my little effort may go a long way in breaking walls of hatred between races, between religions, between castes and between countries. I believe in that.'

'From close quarters? What do you mean by that, Ms T?'

'Promise me to open up after I tell you the whole thing. I am also from Bombay. I underwent a terrible experience in childhood, which I cannot ever forget. I lost my father in a communal clash and we had to flee Bombay, leaving behind all our property and friends.'

'Oh my! Very sad. Your experience is something similar to mine.'

'Similar?'

'Yes. We too left Bombay after a terrible communal clash, in which my father lost his right hand and my sister lost her speech due to shock. Are we talking about the same riots? This was in...'

'How coincidental. Yes. I am also talking about the same riots. The most traumatising event of the riots was that friends turned foes within seconds and did unexpected things. Mobs went mad. You won't believe my father was killed by our own neighbours who were once our best friends. It was just a case of misunderstanding.'

'What? Your own neighbour killed your father? I can't believe that. How can things match so perfectly? My father's hand was cut off by one who used to be his closest friend. This was also a case of misunderstanding.'

Thus the chat went on till 1.30 in the morning and Mr M wrote, 'I have an important surgery tomorrow at 8.30 a.m. I have to go to bed. Let us continue on Sunday next at...'

The next three days, Mehmood's mind kept recollecting his gory past of Bombay. He related all that to Ms T.

****

They were all having dinner, when suddenly there was chaos outside their house. They heard loud noises of some stones breaking windowpanes, people screaming, children crying and dogs barking.

They were just watching the news on TV about a terrible communal clash, which broke out in a bustling chawl when some miscreants pelted stones on a procession being taken out by a religious group. 'They do not deserve to live here. They enjoy all the benefits and yet will not allow us to live in peace,' screamed an angry man on TV to an interviewer.

'We are not safe here. Our own friends are turning foes. They treat us like aliens forever. They don't trust us,' cried another old man.

'Unless they trust us, how can they feel safe? Why can't they mind their own business and not interfere in our activities?' shouted a woman.

Mehmood was just 12 years old then. His sister Zubin was eight and she held on to her mother with fear once she heard the ruckus outside. His brother Shoukat was 18 and he was watching the TV intently.

"Shoukat, come here and look. The street looks like a war field," called Mehmood's father Amjad, anxiously looking out of the small window.

Shoukat ran to the window. By then the crowd – wielding different kinds of weapons like swords, knives, hockey sticks, cycle chains and even rifles – were near the house of Amjad's neighbour. The neighbour Ganpat was standing in the balcony and shouting at the crowd. Mehmood could not hear what Ganpat was saying but could only see him moving his hands left and right, his face red with anger.

The next moment the crowd came pounding on his door. Mehmood and Shoukat stood against the door, the fear of death in their eyes. Amjad shouted: "Begum! Take Mehmood and Zubin and run away through the back door. Go to Zareena's house. We will meet you there."

"No, I cannot leave you in danger. Call Ganpat Bhaiya over phone. He will surely help," the Begum replied, tears rolling down her cheeks.

"Ganpat is a traitor. I saw him giving us up to the crowd. Don't trust these people. Go away!" Shoukat shouted angrily.

Within moments, the weak doors gave way to the force of the angry mob, who stormed into the house. Two men ran towards Amjad who had fallen and was pleading, "Leave us alone! What have we done to you?"

One of them had a sword with which he chopped off Amjad's right hand. Amjad screamed in pain and fell unconscious. Blood flowed all over the floor.

The rampaging crowd broke all the belongings of Amjad. Amidst the mob, Shoukat saw Ganpat screaming and raising his hands with tears as he pushed himself forward. But by then, Shoukat had made up his mind: *This traitor needs to die.* He ran to the kitchen and grabbed the knife. The mob was after him. But he hid himself below the old cot in the storeroom, which was dark.

After some time, he heard the mob moving away, shouting in between, '*Arrey*, spare the lady and the children. We are not brutal like them. The youngster has escaped. We will find him.' Shoukat could only hear the wailing of his mother and Zubin and Ganpat's voice, "Behen, I am so sorry. Don't worry. We will save Amjad Bhaiya. Come, let's take him to the doctor."

"Ammi, don't believe this rascal. He is not a friend," shouted Shoukat and dashing out from his hiding place stabbed Ganpat all over the body.

Everything happened so suddenly. The children were crying loudly. The Begum kept shouting: "Shoukat, come to your senses. Ganpat uncle is our friend."

By then, Ganpat's wife Lalitha and his children Tara and Madan came running to Amjad's house and saw blood all over the floor. They saw Shoukat stabbing Ganpat and ran to his rescue. It was too late. Ganpat was dead.

Shoukat screamed at Ganpat's family. "Tit for tat. That's what you deserve. Take the bloody body and get out of here," and quickly left with his injured father and wailing mother, sister and brother.

That was the last Mehmood saw of Tara, his dear friend and classmate, who was truly an angel. Why did

Shoukat kill Ganpat? Why did Ganpat uncle let them down? Mehmood was totally confused.

They left Bombay and fled to a small village in Assam, where Mehmood's rich uncle lived. Mehmood then left for the US after his MBBS, about 23 years ago. He wondered what happened to Tara and her family.

He was shocked to read the reply, 'I am Tara. Aren't you Mehmood?'

Mehmood's heartbeats could be heard aloud in that silent bedroom. 'Hello! Are you there? I have been looking for you, not for revenge but to explain something to you.'

'Yes. I am here but simply shocked. Is the world so small? Tell me what you want to say.'

'Did you know that your brother Shoukat killed my innocent father hastily? When the crowd came before our house, my father went out and shouted at them: "We are all peace-loving people living here. Why are you behaving like this? Leave us alone."

'Nobody listened to him and somebody in the mob shouted back: "Hey Ganpat, get your friend Amjad out! We want him. Do you know they have killed 24 of our men in Damodar Chawl?"

'"If somebody killed somebody, why do you want to harm my friend? He is a nice man. Go away!" replied my father.

'Since my father did not help them by calling your dad out, they hurled abuses at him, pelted stones at our house, calling us traitors and broke your door open. My father went down and tried to stop the mob, but you know how difficult it is to stop an angry mob. Despite all his efforts, your father was attacked, but we were shocked to see Shoukat stabbing my father. He had totally misunderstood the situation. Circumstances were uncontrollable.

'After you all left, we too left the chawl. My grandfather took us away to Delhi. After my marriage, I came here to Pune. Since then I wanted to clarify to you that my father was innocent and continue my friendship with you. Now, my heart is lighter. Do you agree that a small misunderstanding can lead to lifelong heartbreaks? Let us forget the past and be friends. I invite you to India. I am eager to see your sweet little daughter. Let love survive forever!'

❑❑❑

9

The Anti-climax

Sunil saw the man standing there about a week ago. He was lean, fair, about 5'6" and around 28 years old. He was standing right opposite Sunil's bank, near the post-box, well before the bank opened, and was still there gaping at everyone, even after the bank had closed. Sunil wondered why this man stood there like a log of wood throughout the day!

The next day was salary day for teachers. The bank was heavily crowded. After banking hours, Sunil took a deep sigh and went to relax. He lit a cigarette and just when he lifted his head to enjoy the puff, his eyes fell on the other side of the road. What a strange thing! He saw the same man standing there, gaping at the bank's entrance. Sunil grew suspicious. However, he did not think too much about this even then.

****

On the third day, Sunil was having his tea at around 3 p.m. when he again spotted that man at the same place trying to peep into the bank. On the fourth day, Sunil decided to observe the man closely. That day, he saw the lean man standing with another man, who was of the same age too. But the other man was well built, dark and bespectacled. The lean man was making signs to the other man, who then tried to peep into the bank. But they did not converse. They kept looking at their watches often.

Sunil could not concentrate on his work for the next two days, as the presence of those strangers in front of the bank rang alarm bells in his mind.

****

It was Monday. Sunil came to a decision. He recalled the circular which said that three extra marks would be awarded for promotion to employees who showed extraordinary bravery (risking their lives in catching thieves, dacoits or preventing burglary/dacoity, etc.).

Sunil had everything going for his promotion and he could now add another three marks. But he would not discuss this matter with anyone, lest someone else take the clue and the credit. He would remain alert and catch the thieves himself. So, he kept continuous watch on the two strangers. Definitely, they had some ulterior motive. Otherwise, why the hell would they stand on the road for seven days in succession and observe all the activities at the bank?

On the fifth of every month, the bank made payments to employees of a nearby factory and, therefore,

heavy cash was brought to the branch a day before. It was the fourth and so Sunil was doubly alert. Despite all the din in the branch, he could hear his heartbeat!

It was now around 3.30 p.m. The cash van had arrived. With all the usual precautions, the heavy cash trunk was offloaded from the van. As usual, the uniformed guard looked around with hawkish eyes.

Sunil's eyes were on the two men. Suddenly, the men crossed the road. Both of them had their hands in the pockets. Yes, they were approaching the bank! The trunk was being shifted to the safe room. The two men entered the bank. It was not business time, so there were no customers in the premises. Employees were busy closing the books, tallying and attending to other back-office work.

The Manager and two officers had gone into the safe room to place the cash in the lockers. Sunil's heartbeat quickened. He started sweating. Keeping his eyes locked on the men, whom nobody else seemed to have noticed, he quickly entered the Manager's cabin, ready to press the alarm button.

The two men quietly approached the counter where Prema sat. Prema lifted her eyes and gave a questioning look. One of the men slowly but hesitantly began removing his hand from the pocket, looking around with tension. Sunil's hand was on the alarm button now. The man had just removed his hand when... 'Tring!' went the alarm!

Suddenly, there was commotion. Everyone ran helter-skelter. The guard came rushing out of the safe room with his gun at the ready. Sunil came running out of the cabin and held the lean man by his collar (he dared not take the extra risk of catching the other tough-looking guy – just for the sake of three marks!). The two men could not understand what the sudden commotion was all about. They were clearly confused and frightened. Sunil slapped the lean man and pulled his hand out, which had quickly returned into the pocket, when the alarm rang.

By then, the guard had caught the other man and three employees held the frightened lean man tightly.

But what did they find in his hand? A pistol? Not at all! It contained a pink envelope with a picture of flowers on one corner. Sunil suspiciously snatched the envelope and opened it. He found a neatly written single-page love letter:

Dear Jasmine,

I do not know your real name. But I know you are an unfortunate person like me, who can neither enjoy the musical sound of this earth nor express thoughts verbally. I was in search of exactly such a tender flower like you to be my life partner, for only like minds can make life a success. I too am employed in a bank.

After a wait of seven days, I am taking courage in my hands to approach you. If I am wrong, please forgive me. If not, please respond with just a smile.

Yours lovingly,

Raja

The employees, who had been waiting impatiently while Sunil read the letter, asked him: "What does it say?"

Sunil asked them to release the men and quietly handed the letter to Prema, the deaf-and-dumb clerk. He guiltily looked at her with folded hands and said: "Sorry."

Prema took the letter, looked up at the lean man with recognition and tears in her eyes and, of course, a sweet smile!

❑❑❑

10

Slip of the Tongue

Govinda was shocked to see her in the attire of a widow! Widow at such a young age? How cruel destiny can be! His mind flashed back and remembered her at different stages.

Govinda had begun visiting that temple nearly 15 years ago. He very well remembered that cute, chubby girl who happily dropped coins in the bowls of beggars sitting on the steps leading to the temple. She was accompanied by her parents and brother. She came at least once a week to the temple and every time she found pleasure in giving alms to the beggars. She must have been a girl of 10 or 12 at that time. He somehow felt affectionate towards her and looked forward to the girl's visits.

He saw her bloom into a teenager, but never did that habit of hers change. She then began coming to the

temple with two of her friends. Govinda admired the three girls, who looked pretty and contented. They sometimes came in the mornings, perhaps before they went to their exam halls.

Apart from the regular visits, she would come once a year with a large group of family members. They would offer special *puja* at the temple on that day and serve food specially cooked for the occasion to beggars.

The next scene that flashed before Govinda's mind was the day she came with a smart young man. She looked marvellous in a pink saree and blushed all over as the young man talked to her. Govinda could easily guess that the young man was her fiancé. They then began coming once in two days.

Thereafter, she came with the same man but was now his wife, as the *mangalsutra* around her neck and *sindoor* on the forehead announced. She distributed sweets and clothing to beggars. Govinda was thrilled to see the lovely pair. By then he had almost begun considering her his own daughter and prayed that she always lived happily. She had given meaning to Govinda's drab life, though neither he nor she had ever exchanged a word in all these years.

Then, she stopped coming for a few months and Govinda felt lonely and sad. Had she left the city? Later, she appeared suddenly with an infant in her arms, accompanied by her happy parents and husband. Govinda was relieved. So this was the reason she did not come to the temple for so long! On that day, her husband distributed a packet of sweets and a shawl to each of the beggars.

Thereafter, she came to the temple once a month or so, either with her husband or mother, along with the little son. In between, she did not come for the last two months.

****

Today, she was here with her young son and this attire! How very sad!

"Muniya! Did you observe something? That young lady who gave us alms regularly seems to have lost her husband. How shocking?"

"*Arrey*! Yes, Govinda. I too saw that and felt very sad. She has done so much good to so many of us. But to be rewarded this way..."

The lady now walked out of the temple and began coming down the steps. Her young son joyfully started throwing coins in the bowls of beggars. As they neared Govinda, his heart beat faster and he spoke in a soft voice: "Amma, what is this? What happened to your husband?"

The lady was shocked to hear this and gave Govinda a dirty look. She immediately pulled her son towards herself and without answering his question ran down the steps angrily. Govinda was taken aback...

Suddenly, he remembered his foolishness and adjusted his black goggles guiltily.

❑❑❑

11

Sabari's Story

As Meera teacher entered the class she heard lot of commotion. A few boys in class were shouting at one another and were involved in a scuffle. She was shocked to see young boys of Standard VIII behaving like bad guys shown in movies.

Rapping the duster hard on the table, she shouted, "Will you stop this nonsense. What is this all about?"

The boys were surprised by the teacher's sudden angry outburst and returned to their places, tucking their shirts in and adjusting dishevelled hair.

"Can anyone enlighten me about this unruly behaviour? Do you remember that this is a school, not a goon's den?"

Everybody was silent. "I will not start my lessons unless someone tells me the reason for this bad behaviour.

Come on, quick! Don't waste my time and yours. Your exams are nearing and you will be the losers."

Swaroop stood up slowly, looked around and said, "Ma'am, Ravi and his friends teased Bhima and said he belonged to the scheduled caste and was an untouchable. Bhima was upset and began abusing Ravi. They then started beating each other and the other boys joined in the scuffle."

Ravi glared at Swaroop. Meera teacher noticed this, "Ravi, why are you giving that dirty look? Stand up! I appreciate Swaroop for telling the truth. If I hear any more of this nonsense, I will report the matter to the Principal and see that the culprits are suspended. Apologise to Bhima."

Ravi stood with his head hanging down, but did not obey Meera teacher.

"Keep standing till you realise and accept your mistake. Meanwhile, I will tell you all a story from the *Ramayan*...

"You know how Rama, Lakshmana and Sita went to the forest for 14 years to comply with the orders of King Dasharatha and Queen Kaikeyi. During their stay in the forest, Sita once saw a deer with golden spots and requested Rama to fetch the deer for her. Rama left Sita in Lakshmana's care and went after the deer. But this was simply a deceitful plan of Ravana, the demon king. On hearing the deer calling out to Lakshmana for help in Rama's voice, Sita forced Lakshmana to go to Rama's help, despite Lakshmana's assurance that Rama would be safe. Just as Lakshmana left Sita alone, the cunning Ravana came in the guise of a *sadhu* and kidnapped her. On their return, when Rama and Lakshmana found Sita missing, they were shocked and sad. So they went searching for her throughout the forest when, one day, they met a group of students of a *rishi*, who told the brothers that they were looking for some other ashram, because a woman who was an untouchable served them in the ashram they were staying in before. Rama and Lakshmana were shocked to hear the word 'untouchable' from students of an eminent *rishi*.

"Rama said, 'Of what use is your education if you consider a woman untouchable, when your own mother, sister, wife or daughter are all women? If education has not made you realise that all human beings are equal, there is no point in your going in search of a new ashram.'

"Having said so, the brothers went to the ashram the students had cited and met the so-called untouchable woman, who introduced herself as Sabari. She was an old woman and walked with the support of a walking stick. Rama and Lakshmana were stunned to see her and felt ashamed that the students had deserted an old lady.

"When Rama introduced himself and his brother, Sabari was overwhelmed and offered them tattered leaves to sit upon because that was the only thing in the ashram.

"Rama asked her about her past and she said, 'My son. I am the daughter of a poor hunter from a low caste. When I was to be married, my parents chose a man who sold toddy because that's all they could afford. I did not like him because he was a known drunkard but my parents paid no heed to me. So, one day I ran away from home and came to this forest. I found this beautiful ashram and the *rishi* was a nice man who gave me refuge. I served the ashram collecting firewood, fruits and other necessities and fetching water and keeping the ashram clean. Everybody was happy, until recently, when they discovered I belong to a low caste. They were upset that I had not revealed this to them and they had become unholy by accepting my service. Everyone deserted me. How unlucky are they for they missed God's messengers! I am honoured by your visit, Rama and Lakshmana.'

"'How silly have they been! God sees no discrimination. Every human being is alike for Him. They shall be answerable for their misdeeds,' said Rama.

"'Rama! How unfortunate I am that I have nothing decent to offer you. Ah, yes! I remember. Here are a few fruits that I collected but I do not know whether they are ripe enough for you. I cannot find out unless I taste them. What shall I do?'

"'Mother, why do you worry? You taste them and then give them to us.'

"Sabari was taken aback and cried, 'How can I offer fruits tasted by me, an untouchable?'

"Rama soothed her, 'Mother, that's exactly what I want to disprove. You are not untouchable. Nobody is. Please taste the fruits and give them to us. We are hungry.'

"Sabari then bit each fruit a little, selected the ripe ones and offered them to Rama and Lakshmana very happily. She was pleased to see them eat the fruits with joy. Rama then asked her, 'Mother, what do I offer in return for this tasty meal?'

"'Rama, my son. What does an old, orphaned lady need? You have satisfied my life's ambition by giving your *darshan*. I want *moksha*. I want to leave this wretched world and join the Great Soul. Please grant me this.'

"Sabari's wish was promptly granted. Her great soul discarded the body and left for the heavens.

"What does this story teach? When God Himself has proved that everybody is equal, why do men follow such stupid systems? And you, as children, should take the essence from such scripts and transform yourselves, instead of blindly following others. If you are not gaining good values along with knowledge in schools, there is no use of the degrees you acquire. Ravi, did you understand the message? Will you say sorry now?"

The entire class was silent. Ravi was in tears and said, "Sorry Bhima. Sorry Ma'am. I will never repeat such a thing."

Bhima too was in tears and went and hugged Ravi. "That's okay Ravi. Let us be friends."

"Thank you, Ma'am. We are sorry you could not teach your lessons today," said Bhima.

"No. I am rather happy that I had the opportunity to teach you some good values in life. That's more important than the curriculum," said Meera teacher with satisfaction.

❑❑❑

Children Story Books

3 Vols. • pp: 24 each • Rs. 36/- each
Also available in Hindi

2 Vols. • pp: 56 & 60 each
Rs. 60/- each
Also available in Hindi

2 Vols. • pp: 56 each
Rs. 60/- each. Also available in Hindi

Rs. 36/- • pp: 32
Also available in Hindi

24 pp • Rs. 36/-
Also in Hindi

60 pp • Rs. 60/-
Also in Hindi

48 pp • Rs. 50/-
Also in Hindi

5 Vols. • pp: 60 to 68 each
Rs. 60/- each. Also available in Hindi

Combined Edition
pp: 304 • Rs. 350/-
Also available in Hindi

Postage: Rs. 15/- each book. *Every subsequent book: Rs. 5/- extra*